PUFFIN BOOKS

AMMA, TAKE ME TO THE DARGAH OF SALIM CHISHTI

Bhakti Mathur took to writing in 2010 when she created the popular Amma, Tell Me series of children's picture books about Indian festivals and mythology. After a long stint as a banker, she now juggles her time between her writing, her passion for yoga and long-distance running, and her family. She lives in Hong Kong with her husband, their two children and two dogs. She holds a master of fine arts degree in creative writing from the University of Hong Kong and freelances as a journalist. When not writing or running after her young boys, Bhakti is happiest curled up with a book in one hand and a hot cup of chai in the other. To know more, visit her at www.bhaktimathur.com.

Priyankar Gupta is an animation film designer and visual storyteller. He is associated with various publishing houses as an illustrator for children's books and also works as a pre-visualizer for TV commercials and feature films. He is a visiting faculty member and mentor in various design institutes across the country.

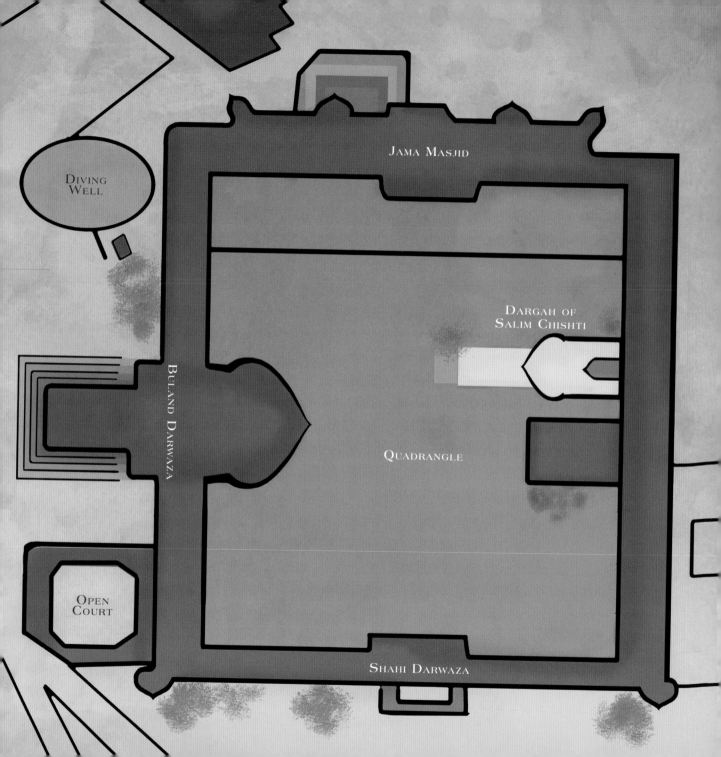

Amma, Take Me to
The Dargah
of Salim Chishti

BHAKTI MATHUR

Illustrations by Priyankar Gupta

PUFFIN BOOKS

An imprint of Penguin Random House

PUFFIN BOOKS

USA | Canada | UK | Ireland | Australia
New Zealand | India | South Africa | China

Puffin Books is part of the Penguin Random House group of companies
whose addresses can be found at global.penguinrandomhouse.com

Published by Penguin Random House India Pvt. Ltd
7th Floor, Infinity Tower C, DLF Cyber City,
Gurgaon 122 002, Haryana, India

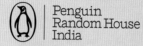

First published in Puffin Books by Penguin Random House India 2018

Text copyright © Bhakti Mathur 2018
Series copyright © Penguin Random House India 2018
Illustrations copyright © Priyankar Gupta 2018

ISBN 9780143428329

Typeset in Agmena Pro
Book design and layout by Neelima P Aryan
Printed at Replika Press Pvt. Ltd, India

www.penguin.co.in

For Peenu Mami—friend, philosopher, guide

 CONTENTS

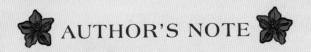 # AUTHOR'S NOTE

The Amma, Take Me series is an attempt to introduce children to the major Indian religions and faiths through their important places of worship. Styled as the travelogues of a mother and her two young children, these books link history, tradition and mythology to bring alive the major temples, churches, mosques and mausoleums of India in an engaging and non-preachy way.

The stories emphasize universal values and the message of love and tolerance central to all faiths. I hope that this journey of Amma and her children will inspire you to embark on your own travels with your children, and I hope that you will enjoy reading these books as much as I enjoyed writing them.

Lastly, these works are a reflection of my personal interpretation of the faith and traditions that these timeless monuments represent. I am far from being an authority on religion or on Indian religious history, and while I have made every effort to ensure that the factual and historical information in these books is correct, I do not assume and hereby disclaim any liability to any party for any loss, damage or disruption caused by errors or omissions.

The countryside stretched out like a great patchwork quilt of golden and green squares, dotted with small brown villages. Lush fields bloomed with mustard flowers. Mango orchards and giant banyan trees, their hanging roots touching the ground, came into sight. Cows grazed lazily under the trees. Next, a local bazaar, with numerous colourful stalls, appeared. The aroma of hot samosas drifted in the air.

Amma was soaking in the sights and smells of the land from the comforts of a taxi. Shiv and Veer sat next to her, busy playing games on their iPad, oblivious to their surroundings. The three were on their way to visit the dargah of Salim Chishti, the mausoleum of the great Sufi saint, situated in the middle of Fatehpur Sikri, the magnificent capital city built by the mighty Mughal emperor Akbar.

'Enough, you two—no more screen time! We haven't come here to play Minecraft,' admonished Amma as she firmly took the iPad from them and put it in her bag.

'That's not fair!' Veer protested. 'I was building a castle. And this ride is *so* long. And *so* boring.'

'Stop whining, Veer. There are lots of interesting things here if you just care to look outside the window,' Amma said. 'How about I tell you a story of a real palace where kings and queens used to live?' she added, trying to liven things up.

'Are you going to tell us about Fatehpur Sikri?' Shiv asked excitedly, knowing that their destination was not too far away. Veer was still grumpy but the prospect of hearing a story was too tempting to resist.

'Yes!' Amma said. 'Are you guys ready to go back 450 years in time?'

Shiv and Veer nodded eagerly.

'Then listen carefully. It's a long story.'

'The year was 1568,' began Amma. 'A strong breeze blew across River Yamuna and over the mighty ramparts of the great red fort that towered over the river and the city of Agra that lay alongside its banks. It was early autumn; the lashing rains and the oppressive heat of the monsoon months had given way to the cool winds blowing in from the mountains in the north.

'Deep inside the great red fort, the imperial court was abuzz with excitement. The most powerful nobles and kings of the land were present that evening. They all seemed to be trying to outdo each other with the magnificence of their costumes, the brilliance

of their jewels and the lavishness of the gifts they had brought to win the favour of their host and ruler, Emperor Akbar, whom people call Akbar the Great. In fact, the word *akbar* means "great" in Persian.'

'You mean they called him Great the Great?' Shiv said with a smirk.

'Yes, Shiv the Shiv!' Veer retorted.

'Oh, stop it, both of you!' Amma said. 'Let me continue.

'They had gathered there to celebrate the anniversary of Akbar's coronation. Everyone marvelled at what the young emperor had achieved in the twelve years since the reins of the Mughal rule had passed into his hands. It had been Akbar's grandfather, Babur, from central Asia, who had won a foothold for the Mughals in India forty years before that, but it was under Akbar that the Mughal dynasty had grown from being masters of a few scattered kingdoms to a vast empire that included almost all of central and northern India.'

'Wow! He ruled over all of India?' Veer asked, awestruck.

'Yes, he did, but instead of rejoicing in his accomplishments, Akbar was miserable and his heart was heavy,' said Amma.

'Why was he sad?' Shiv asked.

'He was unhappy because he had everything and yet he didn't have the one thing he wanted more than anything else—a child. He pondered over the same question for the millionth time. With no heir to succeed him, what would happen to the great empire, which he had forged with his blood and sweat, after his death? Why would God not grant him a child, an heir to carry forward the proud line of his ancestors?'

'What happened then?' asked Shiv.

'Did he have a child?' asked Veer.

'Hold on, you two!' Amma said. 'I haven't finished the story yet.

'Early the next day, disguised as a common soldier, Akbar set out alone towards the village of Sikri, a few hours' ride from Agra. Akbar had heard of a wise and pious man, a Sufi saint by the name of Shaikh Salim Chishti, who lived in Sikri. Heartbroken over not having a child, Akbar decided to visit the saint to seek his blessings. It was thought by many that Salim Chishti could perform wonders and that he had the power to make even the impossible happen. Maybe he could help Akbar, where the other so-called miracle workers had failed.'

'What is a Sufi saint, Amma?' Shiv asked.

'The word *sufi* means "wool" in Arabic, referring to the rough woollen cloaks worn by Sufi sages,' Amma explained. 'Sufis chose a life of meditation and prayer. Sufi saints themselves were disciples of wise masters, whom they called shaikh.'

'That is why Salim Chishti is called shaikh!' Shiv exclaimed.

'Yes indeed, he was a great master,' Amma continued. 'Sufis believe in love and devotion to God. They believe that there is no greater purpose in life than to help others and bring happiness to the human heart. They also believe that love blossoms through poetry and music and that music helps people express their feelings and open their hearts to others. They convey their love for God by singing devotional songs, and this celebration is called *sama*.'

'Do Sufis have a religion?' asked Shiv.

'Sufis are Muslims, who believe that there are many ways of reaching God,' said Amma. 'A great Sufi saint, Nizamuddin Auliya, once saw Hindu worshippers bathing in the Yamuna. He said, *"Har qaum raast raahe, din-e-wa qibla gaahe,"* which means that every community has its own path for finding God.

'Coming back to the story of Shaikh Salim Chishti,' said Amma. 'He had earlier turned down a royal invitation to Agra as the emperor's guest and refused the lavish gifts brought by the royal guard sent to escort him to the imperial court. He had said that there were many people who came for his help every day and he couldn't desert them to be with the emperor. And that he had no use for riches, nor did he want Akbar's gratitude. The captain of the royal guard had been enraged at Shaikh Salim's response and had threatened him with dire consequences, at which the holy man had smiled and gently urged him to do as he pleased.

'*Shaikh Salim is certainly different from others*, Akbar thus thought to himself as he led his horse along the dusty road up the plateau to Sikri. Ahead, in the shimmering heat, he saw the outline of a cluster of mud-brick houses on the edge of the ridge.

'"Do you know where Shaikh Salim Chishti lives?" Akbar asked a villager passing by.

'"Yes, come this way. I am going in the same direction," the man replied, beckoning Akbar to follow him.

'Akbar followed the kind man through the village to a small, low single-storey cottage. The cottage looked so old and shabby that it was surprising how it was still standing. Akbar could see the coarse, uneven bricks that made up the wall. Yet there was something welcoming about it. As he entered, he saw an old man, his eyes closed, his face lined and creased, dressed entirely in robes of rough-spun white cloth, sitting on the floor in deep meditation.

'Akbar waited for him to finish his prayers. Finally Shaikh Salim opened his eyes and saw Akbar. The sage welcomed him with a warm embrace as was his custom. "You seemed to have travelled far. How can I be of service, my son?" he asked.

'Akbar was struck at once by the saint's remarkable eyes. They shone with both wisdom and kindness and had the power to look straight into a man's heart. Akbar felt a sense of calm envelope him and the tiredness from the hard ride earlier in the day seemed to wash away. He folded his hands and said, "I have everything that a man can

wish for, but for a child I so desire. I have heard so much about you. I believe you have the power to help me; please make my wish come true."

"'But you are surely mistaken, my son. I am no miracle worker. Only God and, through Him, you have the power to have a child. There are many roads to God and it is for each one of us to find Him," replied Shaikh Salim.

'Akbar's face fell. "I have come to you with so much faith. Will I have to leave empty-handed from your house?" he asked a little bitterly.

'Shaikh Salim smiled and said, "My years of reflection have taught me that prayer and blessings alone achieve nothing. Love your God, love your fellow man and try to be the best you can be. Your subjects are also your children, Your Majesty. Treat them thus, and I believe God will bless you with one of your own. I will pray for you, my son. Go in peace, Your Majesty."

'Akbar was at first taken aback that the saint had seen through his disguise, but then the wisdom of his words sank in, and he said, "You are right, O wise one. My people are also my children and they need me. I believe that God will fulfil my wishes when you pray for me. When what you say comes to pass, I will found a great city here at Sikri to honour you. Its gardens and fountains and palaces will be a wonder for the world to see, and I will make it the capital of my empire."

'"My biggest honour is in serving people," said Shaikh Salim. "For when I serve people, I serve God. When your wife is with child, send her here. There is a small monastery near the village, where she can live in peace and enjoy the fresh air, away from the noise and distractions of the court."

'"Your wish is my command," said Akbar. "And if I have a son, I will name him Salim after you, O great one." Akbar bowed low to Shaikh Salim, took his blessings and returned to Agra.'

'So, did Akbar have a child?' asked Veer, unable to contain himself.

'Yes indeed, not one, but three—three sons!' said Amma. 'His first son was born a year later. Akbar believed this to be the saint's blessing. When the queen was carrying the child, she went to Sikri and lived in the humble dwelling of the monastery, where she gave birth to a bonny baby boy. As promised, Akbar named the child Salim after the great saint, and he used to affectionately call him Shaikhu Baba.

'Akbar now loved and respected Shaikh Salim tremendously. True to his word, he moved the capital of his empire from Agra to Sikri just to be close to the saint and seek his guidance. Akbar built a magnificent palace in Sikri, which came to be known as Fatehpur Sikri. It was the capital of the great Mughal Empire that stretched from Gujarat in the west to Bengal in the east and to Kabul in the north. Akbar ruled from here from 1571 to 1585,' said Amma. She turned to the boys.

'How many years is that, Veer?' she asked.

'Fifteen, no—sorry—fourteen!' said Veer, changing his reply quickly and looking sneakily at Amma. 'Please don't tell me I need to practise extra maths!' he added before Amma could get a word in.

Amma started laughing. 'We'll see about that later, mister!' She continued. 'Over the next fourteen years, the hills and deserts of Sikri were transformed into a splendid city filled with gardens, elegant palaces and pavilions. Akbar himself selected the site on

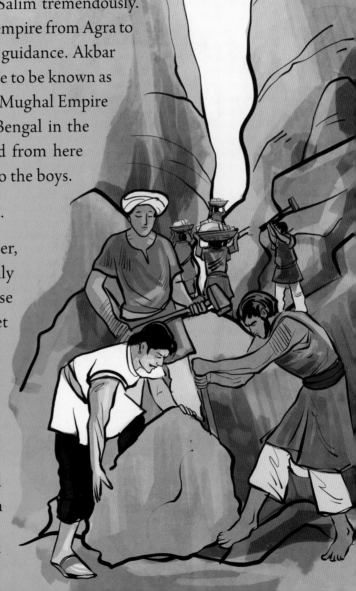

the ridge of the shaikh's village, which had a panoramic view of the area. Eminent architects, masons, stonecutters and sculptors were summoned from all over the empire to construct this city. It is said that it took over 30,000 labourers to build Fatehpur Sikri.

'The top of the hill was sliced off to create a flat area, on which a complex of palaces, pavilions, a mosque, a shrine and courtyards came up with astonishing speed. Huge bazaars—kilometres-long—factories and caravanserais mushroomed at the bottom of the hill. The city was made of red sandstone, which was quarried from the edge of Sikri itself. Akbar wanted to complete the construction of the city as soon as possible. So much so that he carried basketfuls of earth, learnt to cut stone and quarried alongside the stonecutters himself!'

'He worked as a labourer?' Veer asked, surprised.

'Yes!' Amma said. 'This is why Akbar was one of the greatest kings that India has seen. He believed that everyone was equal and that all work should be respected. It also shows how eager Akbar was to build his new capital city!'

The boys listened, wide-eyed.

'Now, let me tell you how Fatehpur Sikri came to be named,' Amma continued. 'The origins of this place go far back in time. Signs of human habitation from as long ago as 1200 BC have been found here. Do you know how many years ago that is?'

Shiv and Veer looked confused.

'About 3200 years ago!' Amma said.

'So long back!' Veer exclaimed.

'Yes, in fact, this place is referred to as Saik in the Mahabharata, meaning "an area surrounded by water", probably a large lake,' said Amma.

'This place is so old!' Veer was impressed.

'It sure is. Did you know Sikri was one of the first places in India to use cannons in a war?' Amma asked.

'Wow!' Shiv cried with excitement.

'When?' Veer asked eagerly.

'In 1527, Babur came to Sikri and camped by the lake before launching an attack on Rana Sangram Singh, the powerful ruler of Mewar. Babur had been attracted to the site because of the ample supply of water for his troops. The two armies finally met in Khanwa, a small village a few kilometres from Sikri. The Mughals triumphed because of their clever military strategies and use of cannons, which destroyed the Rana's army even though it outnumbered the Mughals.

'After the victory, as a gesture of gratitude, Babur renamed the village Shukri, which comes from the Arabic word *shukr*, meaning "thanks to God". The place was much loved by Babur. He built a garden on the banks of the lake and called it Bagh-e-Fath, meaning "garden of victory". In the garden he built a pavilion that he used for writing and relaxing. He also constructed a step-well, known as a *baoli*, and a large platform in the middle of the lake, where he would spend hours writing in his diary.'

'Babur wrote a diary?' asked Shiv. 'Just like me!'

'Yes, he did,' said Amma. 'In fact, his journal entries have been published as a book. It is called *Baburnama*.'

'Can I read it?' asked Veer.

'Of course you can,' said Amma. 'We have it at home. Can you guess what Babur's name means?'

Shiv and Veer shrugged their shoulders.

'Tiger!' said Amma. 'And he was one—a fearless fighter.'

'Can we see the lake and the pavilion Babur made?' Veer asked.

'Sadly they don't exist any more, though there are a few remains on the outskirts of the city that are thought to be the place where the pavilion once stood,' said Amma.

'But let me finish the story about how the city got its name,' said Amma. 'Akbar conquered Gujarat from Sikri, or Shukri as it was called by his father. He felt that the village was lucky for him and renamed it Fatehbad, meaning "the city of victory". Later the village became popular as Fatehpur and, in due course, came to be known as Fatehpur Sikri.

'Barely a year after the construction of the new city started, Shaikh Salim Chishti passed away,' continued Amma. 'The saint was ninety-four years old. Akbar was heartbroken. After all, Shaikh Salim had become a friend and trusted adviser over the years. So Akbar had a beautiful mausoleum built in memory of the Sufi saint. This is known as the dargah of Salim Chishti. Even today people of all faiths, from all over the world, come to seek the blessings of this holy man. That is where we are going, to seek his blessings, too.'

'What is a mausoleum, Amma?' asked Shiv.

'A mausoleum, known as a dargah in Urdu, is a shrine built over the place where a beloved person is buried. People go there to pay their respects, show their love and seek the blessings of the departed soul. The word "dargah" comes from a Persian word that means "portal" or "threshold", where, it is believed, the deceased person's blessings can be sought.

'Do you know the other special thing about dargahs?' asked Amma.

'No,' said Shiv and Veer in unison.

'Where do Hindus go to worship?' asked Amma.

'Temples,' replied Shiv.

'Where do Muslims go to pray?'

'Mosques,' answered Veer.

'That's right,' said Amma. 'But do you know who comes to pray at dargahs?'

Shiv and Veer were silent.

'Both Hindus and Muslims—and people of all faiths, really!' said Amma. 'That is why I love dargahs. They unite people across religions, and I love everything that unites humanity.'

'Why do Hindus and Muslims both go to dargahs?' asked Veer.

'Good question,' said Amma. 'Because Sufis love everyone equally. They see God in every person. It does not matter which religion you belong to, for their religion is to love all. So Hindus and Muslims both feel loved and welcome in dargahs. And who does not like to feel loved? I, for one, certainly do!'

'Amma, when are we going to reach Fatehpur Sikri?' Shiv asked impatiently.

'Soon, soon. We're almost there,' Amma said.

'Shiv, look!' Veer said, pointing to the red sandstone fortress that appeared in the distance, standing majestically atop the hill, as the taxi wound up the steep road.

As they approached, the outline of a massive arched gateway, rising from the hill towards the sky, came into view.

Finally the taxi came to a halt, Amma paid the driver and the three got out. They manoeuvred their way through the prattle of hawkers selling knick-knacks, the chatter of overzealous guides trying to woo them and the bustle of stalls selling tea, snacks and sweets.

'Amma, who are these people?' Veer asked, looking at a few men who seemed to be appealing to Amma.

Amma politely turned them away.

'They are guides who want to show us around Fatehpur Sikri and tell us about the history of the place,' Amma said.

'So why don't we go with them?' Veer asked.

'Because I am your guide today!' Amma said. 'Remember, I told you that I have been coming here since I was a little girl? This must be my seventh trip! The first time I came here was with my grandmother. In fact, I was the same age as you are now, Shiv.'

'Were you naughty, Amma?' Shiv asked with a twinkle in his eyes.

'Not as naughty as you,' replied Amma as she ruffled his hair.

They walked a few steps ahead and stopped. Their eyes followed a steep flight of steps that led to the mammoth structure they had seen on their way up the hill. It was the most impressive building Shiv and Veer had ever laid eyes on. The lofty gateway loomed over them.

'The Buland Darwaza!' Amma said, gazing up at the majestic entrance towering above them.

'Wow!' Veer said in wonder, craning his neck to look up.

Shiv and Veer were astounded and couldn't take their eyes off the imposing doorway. Amma broke their reverie.

'This is the famous Buland Darwaza. It is the main entrance to the palace in Fatehpur Sikri and leads to the dargah of Salim Chishti. The word *buland* means "mighty" and

darwaza means "gate", so Buland Darwaza is the mighty gate. It is 180 feet high—the highest gateway in the world,' said Amma.

'So beautiful and so high!' exclaimed Shiv as Veer looked on in disbelief.

Made of red and buff sandstone, it was decorated with black-and-white marble. The gateway was like a building, of which three sides projected outwards. The main archway, with the entrance, was in the middle. The two other sides had smaller arches—a medium-sized arch, above that a row of smaller arches and then, above that, another smaller arch. A row of tiny *chhatris* (dome-topped pavilions with pillars and arches) ran along the top of each side. They could see many larger chhatris on the roof, the biggest in the middle.

In the hollow of the great central archway were three tiers of smaller arches and ledges. The huge pillars were decorated with intricate patterns and quotes from the Koran.

'This gate was built by Akbar as a symbol of victory to celebrate his conquest over Gujarat,' said Amma. 'It took almost twelve years to build. It is considered to be the greatest architectural achievement of Akbar's entire reign. What a grand sight it must have been—Akbar riding up with his victorious army in tow, amid all the pomp and grandeur, with throngs of cheering people lining the way.'

'You mean he climbed up these very steps?' Veer asked.

Amma nodded.

'Let's run up the stairs, Veer, and count them!' said Shiv as he made a dash for the steps.

'Let's see who reaches first!' Veer said, chasing his brother.

'That was forty-two steps!' he said, panting, as he reached the top of the flight of stairs.

'I won!' said Shiv.

'No, you didn't. You cheated!' complained Veer. 'You started before me.'

'Stop fighting, boys!' said Amma, who was the last to reach, catching her breath.

'Let's look at the Buland Darwaza. What do you see?' she asked, pointing to the roof of the central arch.

'Beehives! So many of them!' Shiv cried, pointing to the numerous honeycombs hanging from the ceiling of the archway.

'And look at this—horseshoes!' shouted Veer, pointing to the black iron-and-wooden door of the gateway.

'Why are there horseshoes on the door, Amma?' asked Shiv.

'These are from many years ago,' said Amma. 'Farmers from the village would come here and nail the horseshoes of their sick livestock, to seek the blessings of Salim Chishti to cure them. They were simple, devoted peasants who loved their animals.

'But look, there is a very interesting quotation on the wall here,' said Amma, pointing to one of the inscriptions engraved on the gateway. 'It quotes Jesus. "So said Jesus, on whom be peace! The world is but a bridge, pass over it, but build no houses upon it. He who hopes for a day may hope for eternity, but the world endures but an hour. Spend it in prayer for the rest is unseen."'

'What does that mean?' asked Veer, puzzled.

'Our life on earth is but a journey, for all of us will die one day; some sooner, some later. So it is foolish to get attached to our belongings, for when we die we are not going to take them with us. Instead we should spend our time wisely, in prayer and contemplation,' explained Amma.

'Was Akbar Christian?' asked Shiv.

'That's a very interesting question, Shiv,' said Amma. 'Akbar was not Christian. He was Muslim. But Akbar had an insatiable curiosity and a great thirst for knowledge. He could not read or write and yet he had a huge library of more than 24,000 books, written in Sanskrit, Persian, Urdu, Greek, Latin and Arabic. He "read" thousands of books on different subjects, including the many religions of the world.'

'How did he read the books if he didn't know how to read?' asked Shiv, looking perplexed.

'He had them all translated into Persian, one of them being the Mahabharata, and had storytellers read them aloud to him. His library had translators, scribes, readers and illustrators,' said Amma.

'He had his own illustrator?' Veer was impressed.

'Not one, but many!' Amma said. 'The calligraphers would copy the manuscript, and then the painters would illustrate them with miniature paintings.'

'Wow!' said Veer. 'Can you become my storyteller, Amma? Then I won't have to read!'

'Very clever, Veer!' Amma said.

'But why couldn't he read?' Shiv asked.

'Because as a child, he was more interested in playing sports. Whenever his tutor came to teach him, he would run away and hide!' Amma said.

Shiv and Veer started giggling.

'But he grew up to become a great scholar, poet and patron of the arts,' said Amma. 'In fact, many famous poets, artists and artisans visited and lived in his court. I think Akbar got his love for books from his grandfather, Babur, and his father, Humayun. The two are known to have carried their precious manuscripts with them, loaded on the backs of camels, during the years they travelled.

'Akbar had a lot of respect for all religions. He said, "All faiths lead to God; then how can one be better than the other?" In fact, he had a building called the Ibadat Khana, meaning "house of worship", constructed here, where he held discussions with philosophers and priests of every religion—Hindus, Christians, Jains, Zoroastrians, Buddhists and more.

'Akbar was inherently tolerant. But he was also shrewd enough to realize that if he wanted to rule in peace, he had to gain the loyalty of all his subjects. His vision of Hindustan was a country whose many religions and cultures, different views and practices would be understood and respected by all.

'His policy of respecting all religions was extraordinary. He saw himself as responsible for the whole population, not just the Muslims. He did a lot to bring Hindus and Muslims together. In fact, he married the daughter of a Hindu Rajput ruler, Bihari Mal, in 1562. She gave birth to Salim, his first son. She was free to practise her religion, Hinduism, all through her life. Akbar also abolished the unfair taxes that used to be imposed on Hindus. This gesture sent the message that to him all his subjects were equal. He even celebrated Diwali and Nowruz, the Parsi new year, every year. At times he even wore a dhoti and put a tilak on his forehead,' said Amma.

'Like a pandit?' asked Veer.

'Yes!' Amma said. 'He appointed Hindus to senior positions in the government and the army, and created an organization that was innovative, efficient and deeply loyal to the king.'

'How do you know so much about Akbar, Amma?' Veer asked.

'Because many books have been written about him, a few of which I have read,' Amma said, 'including a book called *Akbarnama*, Akbar's biography.'

'Just like *Baburnama*?' asked Shiv.

'Yes!' said Amma. 'Except that Babur wrote *Baburnama* himself, while Akbar asked his prime minister and trusted adviser, Abul Fazl, to write his life story. It took Fazl seven years to complete the book.

'Akbar was a legendary warrior and inventive military strategist,' continued Amma. 'Can you guess how many wars he lost?'

'One?' guessed Veer.

'None!' said Amma. 'He never lost a battle, and he fought a lot of battles in the fifty years that he ruled as emperor.'

'How come he never lost a battle?' asked Veer.

'Akbar spent his youth hunting and fighting. That made him a daring warrior,' said Amma. 'The Mughals mastered the techniques of warfare, especially the use of firearms. They used cannons and elephants in war, which proved to be very effective.'

'He ruled for half a century, Amma?' Shiv exclaimed.

'Yes indeed, he did,' Amma said. 'He became king at the young age of thirteen. His father, Humayun, had died suddenly after falling down a flight of stairs—Humayun was only forty-seven years old then.'

'Akbar was a teenager when he became king?' exclaimed Shiv. 'That's just three years older than me!'

'That's true,' said Amma and carried on. 'At the time of Humayun's death, Akbar was in a town called Kalanaur in Punjab, with Bairam Khan, Humayun's trusted adviser. They had been fighting a rebellion there. Akbar was used to fighting battles from a young age. As soon as Bairam Khan received the tragic news of Humayun's demise, he had a stone platform constructed along with a makeshift throne, and had Akbar crowned emperor before anyone else could lay claim to the throne. And you know what, that platform and throne still exist today! It is called Takht-i-Akbari, meaning "the throne of Akbar"'.

'Can we go there? Please, please!' begged the two.

'Some other time. It's not next door, you know! Oh, remember, Akbar loved sports?' said Amma, trying to change the subject.

'Just like me, Amma!' Shiv said.

'Yes, but the sports he liked were a bit different from cricket and tennis,' said Amma. 'He liked riding wild elephants, taming horses and facing tigers in a hunt.'

'That's dangerous!' said Shiv.

'Yes, it is! Akbar was a daring and fearless fighter. Now, let's enter the domain of the great emperor,' said Amma. She led Shiv and Veer to a corner, where they left their shoes for safekeeping before walking through the majestic Buland Darwaza.

The central portico of the door had three arched entrances, with the largest one in the centre. The trio walked through the central hallway that opened into a vast quadrangle made of red sandstone. The quadrangle was enclosed by walls, each more than half a kilometre in length. The walls were lined with rows of evenly spaced columns that supported arches. The arches were topped by parapets with beautiful pavilions. Flanked by a striking mosque, the Jama Masjid, and the towering gateway, the Buland Darwaza, the quadrangle housed one of the most revered sites in India and the one the three had come to see—the dargah of Shaikh Salim Chishti.

Almost as soon as they stepped into the courtyard, a sense of divine tranquillity took over their senses. Even Shiv and Veer were quiet. Maybe it was the soulful sound of the azan coming from the mosque, calling all the faithful to prayer. Or the sight of pigeons taking flight into the clear blue sky. Or the sweet scent of roses wafting in the crisp autumn air.

Then their eyes fell on the dargah in the centre of the courtyard. Made of white marble, the single-storey square mausoleum was breathtakingly beautiful. It stood in the middle of the red sandstone fort like a pearl in the middle of a red sea. It drew the gaze by the sheer splendour of its simplicity. In front of the dargah was a small rectangular pond. It was hard to tell what looked more beautiful—the dargah or its reflection in the clear waters.

'Is that the dargah of Salim Chishti?' asked Veer.

'Yes,' whispered Amma as she gazed at the mausoleum, which looked like a bejewelled casket, the final resting place of Shaikh Salim Chishti.

The three walked across the massive courtyard towards the mausoleum. It was teeming with pilgrims, tourists and local sightseers. Some were walking around, taking in the imposing sight of the Jama Masjid and the Buland Darwaza; some were sitting outside the dargah by the pond, gazing at it lovingly; while others were sitting under a huge tree, enjoying its shade.

Amma covered her head with her dupatta and handed Shiv and Veer two white lace caps to wear.

'Why do we have to cover our heads, Amma?' asked Shiv as he and Veer put on the caps.

'As a mark of respect for the great saint who rests here,' said Amma.

'Just like we did at the Golden Temple,' remembered Veer.

'Yes, that's right,' said Amma.

The dargah rested on a platform that was a metre high. The mausoleum consisted of a dome-topped, square central chamber, surrounded on all four sides by a wide veranda. Delicate marble jali screens enclosed the veranda that was shaded by broad marble eaves running around the tomb. These were supported by a series of eye-catching, finely carved serpentine brackets.

Amma, Shiv and Veer walked up the five steps that led to the entrance of the soothing and welcoming mausoleum. As soon as they entered the dargah, a sense of calm and serenity enveloped them.

Amma beckoned Shiv and Veer to follow her as she stepped inside the passage, walking in the dappled light and shade cast by the breathtakingly beautiful screens.

'Look at the windows,' said Amma softly, stopping in front of one of the intricately carved marble jali windows.

'Isn't this gorgeous?' said Amma in awe, pointing to the window with complex interlocking designs that made the marble look like lace. 'Can you spot any shapes in them?'

'Hexagons!' Shiv said.

'Triangles . . . and stars!' Veer said.

'Did you know that each of these windows has been carved out from a single piece of marble?' Amma said.

'Wow! That must have been hard!' Shiv said, touching the cool marble.

'Yes! They were incredibly talented craftsmen,' Amma said.

'Look, Amma, the sunbeams are making hexagons on the floor,' said Veer, pointing to the sun's rays shining through the latticed windows, creating honeycomb patterns on the floor and lending a mysterious aura to the dargah.

Amma nodded. It was no wonder this place was a delight for photographers.

The three made one round of the gallery around the saint's tomb, stopping to admire the intricately carved windows time and again. Finally they entered the tomb chamber through an arched doorway, finely carved and painted, over which were carved the names of Allah and Prophet Muhammad, flanked by painted flowers and creepers. Below it was a line inscribed in Persian, mentioning the year of the shaikh's death: 1572. There was also a couplet in Persian, in praise of Shaikh Salim: 'The flame of the House of Chishti is bright on account of him; he is the most worthy descendant of Farid Ganj-i-Shakar in piety and charity.'

The floor of the central chamber was paved with white marble that was inlaid with multicoloured stones, and the walls had intricate floral designs in green and red. Dim light filtered through the rows of screens and the sweet fragrance of agarbattis filled the air. A hush fell over all of them.

In the middle lay the tombstone of the great Sufi saint. A beautiful canopy rose over the tomb, carved out of ebony and inlaid with glistening mother-of-pearl, held up by

four elegant columns with elaborate capitals (large decorative pillar heads). Both the inner and outer walls of the sanctum were engraved with inscriptions from the Koran.

The chamber was filled with people. Some were reverently laying colourful *chadar*s on the tomb, some were gently placing flowers on the tombstone, while others were tying red-and-yellow threads on the latticed screens of the windows, which were already full of countless strands. A group of women wearing saris received a blessing from the tomb keeper with a brush of bound peacock feathers. Love and devotion was writ large on the faces of the pilgrims.

The pervasive presence and blessings of Salim Chishti could be felt in the small hall that housed his remains. Shiv and Veer stood quietly as Amma bent down to place flowers on the tombstone.

'Why are people tying threads on the windows?' asked Shiv.

'Shh,' Amma whispered. 'I will tell you once we are outside.'

The three spent a few quiet moments in the dargah and then stepped outside.

'Come, let's sit here,' said Amma, pointing to a corner outside the dargah, next to the pond.

They sat gazing at the dargah for a while, watching people entering with their heads covered, colourful flowers in their hands.

'Once this was nothing but barren land and wilderness, a place where Salim Chishti used to spend hours meditating,' said Amma, looking at the dargah.

'You mean there was a jungle here, with wild animals?' Veer said.

'Yes indeed. In fact, the Mughal emperors used to go hunting in the forest,' said Amma. 'The dargah was built almost 500 years ago. The mausoleum was originally built of red sandstone and a little bit of marble. It was during Akbar's son Salim's rule that the mausoleum was decorated with marble. The dome was covered in marble later on, under British rule. But I have no doubt that the dargah looked just as beautiful when it was first erected in simple sandstone as it does today.

'Let me tell you a bit about this great Sufi saint,' Amma said. 'Shaikh Salim descended from a long line of Sufis, whose origins in India began with a great Sufi master by the name of Moinuddin Chishti. Moinuddin Chishti was from Persia, and he visited Bukhara and Samarkand during his travels, then went to Lahore for a short period and from there he came to Ajmer and settled down, towards the end of the twelfth century. One of Moinuddin Chishti's disciples was Baba Farid Ganj-i-Shakar, who went on to become a famous Sufi saint. He was also one of Salim Chishti's ancestors. In fact, his name is written on the wall of the dargah too.

'Born in Delhi in 1479, young Salim Chishti moved to the town of Sikri with his father. He went on his first pilgrimage to Mecca when he was in his forties. He returned to India after a decade and lived in a small cottage on the barren ridge of Sikri. After another long journey abroad, he returned for good to Sikri and started a small hospice—a shelter for travellers and those in need. His generosity and love attracted large crowds and he would be surrounded by the poor, simple stonecutters of Agra. They paid homage to him by building a small mosque nearby. In fact, this mosque was built even before Akbar came to Sikri.'

'Can we see the mosque?' asked Veer.

'Yes, of course,' said Amma.

'Amma, why were people tying threads on the windows inside?' asked Veer.

'It is believed that by tying a thread, or *dhaga*, and making a wish here, your wish will come true. And when your wish comes true, you have to come back and untie a thread as a way of giving thanks,' Amma said as she walked towards a window and started untying two threads.

'The threads are thought to be constant reminders to the saint to grant us our wishes. Perhaps they are a constant reminder to us of our strongest, deepest desires,' Amma said.

'Really? Is that true? I am going to wish for a helicopter operated by a remote control!' exclaimed Shiv.

'I am going to wish for movie night every night,' piped up Veer.

'Let me tell you something, boys. As a little girl, with her head full of dreams, when I first visited the dargah, I thought the Sufi saint was some sort of

a magician, a superhero of sorts, who could make anything happen. Years later, I have come to realize that the real hero lies within us, that we already have everything within us to turn our dreams into reality. The act of tying the thread is a way of seeking the saint's blessings to give us the strength to work hard and for our endeavours to bear fruit. So no one else can make your dreams come true. Only you can!' Amma said.

'And if you are going to watch movies every night, Veer, I doubt that your dreams will ever come true!' she added.

'Why did you untie two threads?' asked Shiv.

'Because I had made two wishes the last time that I was here and they both came true!' Amma replied.

'What did you wish for?' both the boys asked.

'For you—and you!' Amma said, looking at the two boys one by one.

'Really?' said Shiv as he and Veer reached over to hug Amma.

Just then, a group of eight men appeared. Some of them had long, flowing white beards, while the others were younger. One of them carried a harmonium, another a dholak. They were all dressed in long kurtas, their heads covered with caps. They sat in two rows, facing the dargah. The man in the middle, the lead singer, started singing while playing the harmonium. The notes of 'Maula Salim Chishti, Aaqa Salim Chishti' floated in the air. Soon the other singers joined in, singing in unison, clapping their hands rhythmically. The song built towards a crescendo, enrapturing everyone around. By now, people had gathered around them and were listening intently. The powerful,

poetic and transcendent music filled the air. Shiv and Veer were enthralled, even though they could not understand the meaning of the song.

After a while, Shiv asked, 'Amma, what are they singing?'

'They are singing a qawwali,' Amma said. 'It is in praise of Salim Chishti. Qawwali comes from the Arabic word *qaul*, which means "to speak". It is a form of devotional music by which you express your love for God through poetry and singing. God is very often referred to as the beloved in these songs.'

'Is this the sama that you told us about earlier?' asked Veer.

'Well done!' Amma said. 'Yes, it is. But it is nothing compared to the celebration that happens on the death anniversaries of Salim Chishti and other Sufi saints. The death anniversary of a Sufi saint is called *urs*, the Arabic word for "wedding".'

Shiv and Veer looked puzzled.

'The death of a Sufi is not mourned but is cause for celebration as it suggests a return of the individual soul to its source, like a stream that merges into the ocean,' explained Amma. 'There is singing and dancing around the tomb, and often devotees go into a trance that makes them more aware of their relationship with God.

'The first time I heard a qawwali was at this very same spot. I was ten years old and was as mesmerized as the both of you are. Who knows, maybe some of the men singing today may have been singing at that time too, when I was here as a little girl, and maybe their ancestors sang when Emperor Akbar visited the shrine to pay his respects.'

Shiv and Veer were quiet.

'I want to show you two more beautiful monuments,' continued Amma. 'Look to your left.'

'A mosque!' said Shiv.

Made of red sandstone, the mosque had three arched openings framed by panels and crowned by chhatris. The central mihrab (the niche in the wall that pointed towards Mecca) was adorned with glazed mosaic, with golden inscriptions on a royal-blue background.

'Yes! That is the Jama Masjid,' said Amma. 'It was the first monument to be built here, the largest mosque of its time in the country. Akbar himself directed the building of the mosque. He used to pray here regularly, and was often seen sweeping the floors. That's how devoted he was.'

'Can we go inside?' asked Veer.

'Yes. We will, soon,' said Amma. 'It is beautiful from the inside as well.

'The other monument I want to show you,' Amma said, pointing to a massive gateway on the right, 'is the Shahi Darwaza, meaning "the emperor's gate".'

Shiv and Veer's gaze followed Amma's finger to a huge ornate doorway.

'This gate was used by Akbar to enter the courtyard to go to the mosque or to pay his respects at Salim Chishti's dargah,' said Amma.

The three sat quietly, taking in the splendour of the dargah flanked by the Jama Masjid on one side and the Shahi Darwaza on the other, with the Buland Darwaza looming behind them.

'Amma, where is Akbar's palace?' asked Shiv.

'Right behind this complex,' said Amma. 'We are going to see it soon. It is called the Khwabgah, meaning "the palace of dreams". There are lots of other interesting things to see as well—the palaces of Akbar's queens; a pond called Anup Talao; Akbar's private meeting room, called the Diwan-i-Khas; and his public meeting room, called the Diwan-i-Aam.'

'Let's go!' said Veer impatiently.

'One minute, Veer,' said Amma as she looked at Shiv, who was tugging at her dupatta.

'I have one question, Amma,' said Shiv. 'You told us Akbar ruled for fifty years, and that he ruled from here for fourteen years. Remember, Veer? You did the maths. Why did Akbar leave Fatehpur Sikri?'

'That's an interesting question. One that remains a mystery to this day,' said Amma.

'Historians give different reasons. Some say the lake here dried up, which caused a shortage of water. That made the city difficult to live in. The more likely reason, given by others, is that Akbar left with his army to fight his stepbrother, who had attacked Punjab. After that, Akbar fought one Afghan tribe after another, conquering Kashmir and Sind. He moved to Lahore and ruled from there for seventeen years, which probably made more sense for him since there was so much unrest in the area. He did return to Agra but not to Fatehpur Sikri. Instead he ruled from Agra Fort.'

'Why was that?' asked Shiv.

'He was growing old. His oldest son, Salim, was rebelling against him. Akbar probably felt safer in Agra Fort, which housed the imperial army and the treasury.'

'Why did his son rebel against him?' Veer asked.

'Because he wanted to dethrone his father and become king,' said Amma.

'But how could he fight his dad?' Veer said.

'I'll remind you of this the next time you argue with your dad!' said Amma, caressing his cheek affectionately. 'It is the desire for power, Veer. It makes son fight against father and brother against brother. The son for whom Akbar prayed and sought the blessings of Shaikh Salim Chishti, the son whose birth he celebrated by building a city—the same son rebelled against him. Isn't that sad?'

Shiv and Veer were quiet for a few minutes.

'You mean if dad were an emperor, Shiv and I would fight with each other for the throne?' asked Veer, breaking the silence.

'Probably,' said Amma. 'You fight over everything you have, anyway, don't you?'

Shiv and Veer started laughing.

'C'mon, I want to see Akbar's palace!' said Veer.

'No, I want to go to the mosque first!' said Shiv.

'Okay, okay!' said Amma. 'But there is one last thing I want to tell you. Akbar's rule from Fatehpur Sikri was special. These were the golden years of his reign. He ruled over a

vast empire, fought countless battles from here and yet he found time for the things that he had a passion for—he spent time listening to musicians like Tansen sing and poets like Faizi recite poetry, as well as admiring miniature paintings produced by the best artists. He even found time to spend alone, meditating by himself, sitting on a stone slab.

'Life should be like that, Shiv and Veer,' said Amma.

'You mean we should all be kings?' said Veer with a naughty look in his eyes.

'You both are already my little princes!' said Amma. 'What I mean is that you must do the things that you enjoy, that you have a passion for. That's what makes life rich and worth living.' She ruffled their hair, got up and started walking towards the Jama Masjid.

Shiv and Veer followed.

The dargah stood silent, as beautiful as ever, sending out its blessings.

THE MUGHAL DYNASTY

Babur (1483–1531)

Jahangir (1569–1627)

Shah Jahan (1592–1666)

Humayun (1508–1556)

Akbar (1542–1605)

Aurangzeb (1618–1707)

Bahadur Shah Zafar (1775–1862)

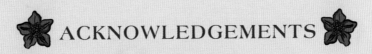 ## ACKNOWLEDGEMENTS

Writing this book has been quite the journey, and I have been lucky in my fellow travellers, who have unstintingly supported me every step of the way.

My husband, Anurag, who supports me with an unwavering love and generosity that I am grateful for every day and without whom this book would have been a jumble of notes in my writing pad.

My little men, Shiv and Veer, who bring me so much joy. I hope that this book can be an answer to some of your whys, hows and whens.

My aunt Tanuja, for giving so freely of her love and time. And for making the trip to Fatehpur Sikri so memorable. I can never thank you enough for all that you have done.

Sohini Mitra, my fantastic editor at Penguin, for coming up with the idea for the series and convincing me to write it. I am so happy that you didn't give up on me.

The team at Penguin India, who worked tirelessly on this book.

To the wonderful members of the Society of Children's Book Writers and Illustrators—John, Larry, Mio, Rachel and Ritu—for being such enthusiastic readers of my drafts and for encouraging me to find my voice.

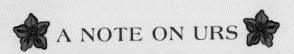 A NOTE ON URS

Urs is the death anniversary of a Sufi saint, celebrated at the saint's dargah with much love and enthusiasm every year. The word urs comes from the Arabic word *uroos*, meaning 'the ultimate meeting with God'. Dargahs become destinations of huge crowds of pilgrims, who arrive from all over the country and even from overseas. It is a period charged with divinity, observed by both Hindus and Muslims, men and women, the rich and the poor, as they express their devotion and affection for the Sufi saint.

All through the day devotees offer prayers. There are continuous colourful processions of pilgrims offering beautiful floral coverings, or chadars, for the mazar, or tomb. Some devotees walk towards the dargah with the chadars folded over their heads, while others elaborately display them all the way. Then they spread them lovingly over the mazar. Musicians sing qawwalis, the beats of drums fill the air and people sing *bandhawa*s. The bandhawa is a specialized form of plain singing that is unique to the urs celebrations. No musical instruments are used; instead rhythm is given to the recitals by clapping. The singing and clapping rises to a crescendo as the devotees' fervour increases.

Bazaars selling knick-knacks spring up all around. Delicious kheer, garnished with dry fruit, is cooked in a massive pot and distributed among the people. The urs of Khwaja Moinuddin Chishti in Ajmer is one of the most famous urs festivals around the world, attracting more than 4,00,000 devotees each year.

SUFI ORDERS AND THE DARGAHS OF
FAMOUS SUFI SAINTS IN INDIA

Sufi saints, commonly known as shaikhs, belonged to the mystical Sufi communities that originated in Iran, Iraq and central Asia from the ninth century onwards. The impact of Sufism in India was felt towards the end of the twelfth century.

Many Sufi saints migrated to Sind, Punjab, Rajasthan, Delhi, Bihar, Bengal and the Deccan, where they established the various Sufi orders, or *silsilas*—Chishti, Suhrawardi, Qadiri, Firdausi, Qubrawi, Shattari, Naqshbandi and more. These orders flourished in India because of the influential teachings of the saints and their spiritual successors, known as *khalifa*s.

The Suhrawardi fraternity was known for its spiritual as well as literary and educational traditions. It gained prominence under Shaikh Bahauddin Zakariya in the early thirteenth century and established itself in Bihar, Bengal and, later, in Gujarat. The Qadiri order, known for the wisdom, eloquence and piety of its founder, Shaikh Abd al-Qadir Jilani, became popular in Sind, Kashmir and the Deccan.

The most popular and widespread silsila, however, was the Chishti order, the one with the largest number of followers to date. It was established in Ajmer by Khwaja Moinuddin Chishti after his arrival in India in 1192. A large number of people were drawn to him because of his sincerity, kindness and devotion. Affectionately called Garib Nawaz, 'patron of the poor', he used to say that a true Sufi should possess 'generosity like that of the river, affection and kindness like that of the sun and humility like that of the earth'.

The everlasting allure of the dargahs is owed to the extraordinary shaikhs who are commemorated there. Even today, people are drawn to their innate spirituality, loving and kind nature, modest living, wisdom and the hospitality of their *khanqah*s, or shelters for Sufi travellers and the needy. These saintly qualities have lived on after their deaths, radiating as blessings, or *baraka*, from their graves.

Kings and rulers often became personal disciples of particular saints and made pilgrimages to their dargahs. They even had themselves buried near their spiritual masters. Jahanara, daughter of the Mughal emperor Shah Jahan, is buried near the grave of Hazrat Nizamuddin Auliya in Delhi. Aurangzeb, the last of the great Mughals, chose one of the dargahs in Khuldabad as his last resting place.

A list of famous dargahs in India:

* **Dargah of Khwaja Moinuddin Chishti (d. 1236), Ajmer**
  Ruler: Sultans Qutbuddin Aibak and Shamsuddin Iltutmish

* **Dargah of Hazrat Nizamuddin Auliya (d. 1325), Delhi**
  Ruler: Khalji and Tughlaq sultans

* **Dargahs of Shaikh Burhanuddin Gharib (d. 1337) and Shaikh Zaynuddin Shirazi (d. 1369), Khuldabad**
  Ruler: Sultan Muhammad bin Tughlaq and Bahmani sultans Alauddin Hasan and Muhammad I

* **Dargah of Shaikh Sharfuddin Maneri (d. 1381), Bihar Sharif**
  Ruler: Sultan Muhammad bin Tughlaq

* **Dargah of Hazrat Khwaja Banda Nawaz Gesu Daraz (d. 1422), Gulbarga**
  Ruler: Bahmani sultan Tajuddin Firuz

* **Dargah of Makhdum Ali Mahimi (d. 1431), Mahim**
  Ruler: Sultan Ahmed Shah I

* **Dargahs of Shaikh Ahmad Khattu (d. 1446) and Hazrat Shah Alam (d. 1475), Ahmadabad**
  Ruler: Sultans Ahmed Shah I, Qutbuddin Ahmad II and Mahmud Begada

- **Dargah of Hazrat Shahul Hamid (d. 1558), Nagore**
  Ruler: Vijayanagara ruler Achyutappa Nayak

- **Dargah of Shaikh Salim Chishti (d. 1572), Fatehpur Sikri**
  Ruler: Mughal emperor Akbar

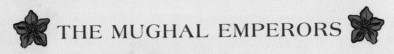 THE MUGHAL EMPERORS

The Mughal Empire lasted from 1526 to 1857. The first six kings—Babur, Humayun, Akbar, Jahangir, Shah Jahan and Aurangzeb—ruled over an empire that covered most of the Indian subcontinent and parts of Afghanistan. After the death of Aurangzeb in 1707, the empire started declining and, by the end, the huge empire built by Akbar was reduced to just the area around Delhi. In 1857, the last Mughal king, Bahadur Shah II, was dethroned by the British and banished to Rangoon, Burma (present-day Myanmar).

The empire was started by Babur. He traced his ancestry to two conquerors—the Mongol Genghis Khan and the Chagatai Turk Timur, who ruled Persia. The Mughals called themselves Timuriya after the Persian king. The Mughal dynasty was also very proud of its Persian lineage and introduced Persian traditions in their art, architecture and court etiquette. They came to be called Mughals, an adaptation of the word 'Mughul', the Persian word for Mongol.

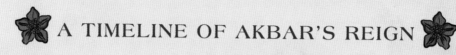

A TIMELINE OF AKBAR'S REIGN

- **15 October 1542** Birth of Jalaluddin Muhammad Akbar in Umerkot, Sind (modern-day Pakistan)

- **1555** Humayun is restored to the throne of Delhi.

- **26 January 1556** Death of Humayun

- **14 February 1556** Akbar ascends the throne at age thirteen

- **5 November 1556** The Second Battle of Panipat, in which Hemu is defeated by Akbar and Bairam Khan

- **1560** Bairam Khan rebels but surrenders to Akbar.

- **1562** Akbar marries the daughter of Raja Bihari Mal of Amer.

- **1564** Discriminatory tax (*jizya*) on Hindus is abolished.

- **1565–73** Construction of the fort in Agra

- **1568** Akbar meets the Sufi saint Salim Chishti in Sikri and asks for his blessings to have children.

- **1569** Work starts in Sikri, on a mosque and a seminary.

- **30 August 1569** Birth of Akbar's first son, Salim

- **7 June 1570** Birth of Akbar's second son, Murad

- **1571** Akbar decides to build a new capital in Sikri.

- **10 September 1572** Birth of Akbar's third son, Daniyal

- **1572** Akbar conquers Gujarat.

* **1573** The village of Sikri is renamed Fatehpur Sikri.

* **1575** The Ibadat Khana is founded in Fatehpur Sikri.

* **1580** Akbar permits Hindus who were forcibly converted to Islam to revert to Hinduism.

* **1582** Akbar promotes his new religion, Din-i-Ilahi.

* **1586** Akbar leaves Fatehpur Sikri. He goes on an expedition to Punjab and is based in Lahore for the next seventeen years. On his return, he settles in Agra Fort, which remains his headquarters till his death.

* **1600** Prince Salim makes an unsuccessful attempt to seize Agra.

* **1602** Prince Salim declares himself king in Allahabad, but this rebellion also fails.

* **25 October 1605** Death of Jalaluddin Muhammad Akbar. Salim becomes the emperor, with the title Jahangir.

A TIMELINE OF SALIM CHISHTI'S LIFE

* **1479** Birth of Salim Chishti. He moves to Sikri with his family soon after.

* **1524–25** Begins a pilgrimage to Mecca and remains there for thirteen years, visiting Iraq, Syria, Turkey and Iran

* **1537–38** He returns to Sikri and begins living on the uninhabited ridge that will later become the site of the Mughal capital Fatehpur Sikri. His saintliness and devotion result in Sikri becoming a centre for the Sufis and the poor.

* **1554–63** Travels to Mecca again and lives there

* **1563** At eighty-four years of age, he returns to Sikri for good and constructs a khanqah for the poor.

* **1568** Akbar hears about the pious saint and pays him a visit in Sikri. The saint predicts the birth of Akbar's three sons.

* **1569** Birth of Akbar's first son, who is named Salim after Salim Chishti

* **1572** Death of Salim Chishti

* **1581** Work on Salim Chishti's tomb is completed. It is built with a mix of red sandstone and marble, with the veranda and dome in red sandstone.

* **1606** Salim's foster brother Qutbuddin Khan Koka adds the exquisite marble screens and the marble floor.

* **1866** The dome is clad in marble by the district magistrate of Agra, using the funds of the mausoleum.

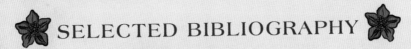

SELECTED BIBLIOGRAPHY

❀ Currim, Mumtaz and George Michell, eds. *Dargahs: Abodes of the Saints*. Marg Publications, 2004.

❀ Dehlvi, Sadia. *Sufism: The Heart of Islam*. Harper Collins Publishers India, 2009.

❀ Eraly, Abraham. *Emperors of the Peacock Throne: The Saga of the Great Mughals*. Penguin Books India, 2000.

❀ Eraly, Abraham. *Mughal World: India's Tainted Paradise*. Phoenix, 1997.

❀ Fazl, Abu'l. *The Akbar Nama of Abul Fazl*. Translated by H. Beveridge. Low Price Publications, 2010.

❀ ———. *The History of Akbar: Volume 1*. Edited and translated by Wheeler M. Thackston. Harvard University Press, 2015.

❀ Foster, William. *Early Travels in India: 1583–1619*. Humphrey Milford, Oxford University Press, 1921.

❀ Gaur, R.C. *Excavations at Fatehpur Sikri*. Aryan Books International, 2000.

❀ Goel, Vikram Chandra. *Fatehpur Sikri: The City of Victory and Harmony*. Kitab Mahal, 2000.

❀ Gupta, Subhadra Sen. *Fatehpur Sikri: Akbar's Magnificent City on a Hill*. Niyogi Books, 2013.

❀ Havell, E.B. *A Handbook to Agra and the Taj, Sikandra, Fatehpur-Sikri, and the Neighbourhood*. Longmans, Green and Co., 1904.

❀ Hiro, Dilip, ed. *Babur Nama: Journal of Emperor Babur*. Translated by Annette Susannah Beveridge. Penguin Books India, 2006.

- Hoyland, J.S., trans. The Commentary of Father Monserrate, S.J.: On His Journey to the Court of Ak*bar*. Humphrey Milford, Oxford University Press, 1922.
- Jaffer, Mehru. *The Book of Muinuddin Chishti*. Penguin Books India, 2008.
- ———. *The Book of Nizamuddin Aulia*. Penguin Books India, 2012.
- Mehta, Jaimini. *Embodied Vision: Interpreting the Architecture of Fatehpur Sikri*. Niyogi Books, 2014.
- Peck, Lucy. *Fatehpur Sikri: Revisiting Akbar's Masterpiece*. Roli Books, 2016.
- Rezavi, Syed Ali Nadeem. *Fatehpur Sikri Revisited*. Oxford University Press, 2013.
- Smith, Vincent A. *Akbar: The Great Mogul, 1542–1605*. Clarendon Press, 1917.
- Verma, Chob Singh. *Splendour of Fatehpur Sikri*. Agam Kala Prakashan, 1999.

READ MORE IN THE SERIES

Amma, Take Me to the Golden Temple

COME, EXPLORE THE PLACES WHERE WE WORSHIP!

Join Amma and her children as they travel to the famous Golden Temple in Amritsar, the holiest seat of Sikhism.

Take a tour through the wonderful sights and sounds of Harmandir Sahib. Hear inspiring stories about the Sikh gurus. Discover the rich heritage of the Darshani Deori and the Akal Takht. Take a sip from the sacred waters at Har ki Pauri and savour the hearty langar offered by the world's biggest kitchen. Learn Guru Nanak's eternal message of equality, love and service. Listen to Amma with your eyes and ears wide open, for this whirlwind of a journey promises to leave you mesmerized!

Told through interesting stories with captivating illustrations, this new series introduces readers to the history of different faiths and their associated monuments that draw thousands and thousands of enthusiastic visitors every day.

'Contains a wealth of detail . . . The lively text is complemented by excellent illustrations' *The Hindu*

'A treat of a read. [The] illustrations . . . make the narrative sparkle and [make] us eager for the rest of the series' *Indian Express*

'Beautifully weaves the intricate history and different aspects of Sikhism in the narration' *Asian Age*

READ MORE IN THE SERIES
Amma, Take Me to Tirupati

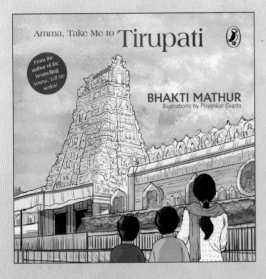

COME, EXPLORE THE PLACES WHERE WE WORSHIP!

Travel with Amma and her boys to the famous Sri Venkateswara Swamy Temple in Tirupati.

Enjoy the drive up the lush green hills of Tirumala while listening to the story of how a divine snake became a hill range. Find out how Vishnu came to reside in the very same peaks, first as a boar and then as a heartbroken husband. Blend into the hustle and bustle of thousands of adoring devotees. Relish a few quiet moments by Lake Swamy Pushkarini. Wake up bright and early to the hymns of Suprabhatam to see Venkateswara in all his glory. Savour the delicious Tirupati laddu as prasad. Listen to Amma with your eyes and ears wide open, for this whirlwind of a journey promises to leave you mesmerized!

Told through interesting stories with captivating illustrations, this new series introduces readers to the history of different faiths and their associated monuments.

'Mathur has a fine eye for detail and strikes a perfect balance between history, folklore, information and anecdote' *Indian Express*